Anonymous

The Polisher Miloch

Anonymous

The Polisher Miloch

ISBN/EAN: 9783337292720

Printed in Europe, USA, Canada, Australia, Japan

Cover: Foto ©Thomas Meinert / pixelio.de

More available books at **www.hansebooks.com**

THE POLISHER MILOCH;*

OR,

THE DREADFUL CONSPIRACY.

BY

⁎   ⁎   ⁎

A

𝔐𝔲𝔰𝔦𝔠𝔞𝔩, 𝔚𝔬𝔣𝔲𝔩, 𝔞𝔫𝔡 𝔗𝔢𝔞𝔯-𝔓𝔯𝔬𝔳𝔬𝔨𝔦𝔫𝔤 𝔗𝔯𝔞𝔤𝔢𝔡𝔶.

IN THREE ACTS.

"If you have tears,
Prepare to shed them now."

* The Polish King.

New-York :
JOHN A. GRAY, PRINTER, STEREOTYPER, AND BINDER,
CORNER OF FRANKFORT AND JACOB STREETS,
FIRE-PROOF BUILDINGS.

———

1860.

RESPECTFULLY DEDICATED TO AND WRITTEN FOR

The Doughty Knights of the Round Table,

BY THEIR

SCRIBE AND POET-LAUREATE.

Augusta, Ga. 1858.

DRAMATIS PERSONÆ.

COUPLE 1st.—King of Poland, an indulgent monarch, indulging his subjects with occasional displays of temper, and himself with plenty of sleep and lager beer.

HIGH PRIEST—("The head and front of the offending,") an out-and-out Snarleyow.

HERR GENTLE BRUTE—(Gentle but in name; his ambition only equalled by his hatred to the King and the King's English.)

COL. SCHWITZER—Commander-in-Chief of the Francifoos Guards, who can command the Guards, but not his perspiration.

LORD LUTHER GAB—A well-drinking, well-spoken, well-meaning, and self-conceited gentleman.

CHAMBERLAIN—A strong adherent alike to Cupid and to Couple.

SIR ARNOLD DOODLESACK—Knight, Minister Plenipotentiary from the Court of Bavaria, an overdone and most incorrigible dum.

WILHELMINA—An enthusiastic, romantic, bombastic, and very sensitive young lady, with a small fortune, but a large heart.

Motley Brothers, Courtiers, Soldiers, Knights, (both foreign and domestic,) Bavarian Pages, brooms, glasses, handcuffs, and lager beer—by the entire strength of the Company.

KING COUPLE.

ACT I.

SCENE I.—*A Room in the Palace.*

Table, Chairs, and Sofa.

Enter KING AND HIGH PRIEST.

King. It is very goot, vat you do say,
But in dis ting I'll have my way.
Vat I vant, and it is said,
Must by all mine subjects be obeyed.
Now mine goot fellow, list to me,
And much wiser vill you be.
For as a great king must be kind,
I now " vill give you a piece of my mind."
The dispute vich you and mine oder subject
Have beswishen you, must be dropped.
Must ; ven I say must, let none dare
To disobey ; for bad will fare
That subject, who doesn't sneeze
Ven I takes snuff.   Now if you please,
Shust leave mine majesty mit mineself, alone,
For mine eyes feel heavy as a mill-stone ;
And my mouth, which I can't command—oh !
   tear, (*yawns*)
Keeps stretching open from ear to ear.
H. P. Most potent, grave, and contemptible sire,
Suspend for a while your anger and ire,

Until I most humbly and briefly relate,
The many mishaps of my terrible fate.
I—

King (interrupting).
Hush mit your fate; what's it to me.
Didn't I say before, that I was sleepy ?
Take care, don't worry me any more;
I'm sleepy—I believe I've said so before.

H. P. Your majesty cuts my woful tale off,
Which—

King (interrupting).
I'll cut off your tale and your kopf*
If you don't cut your sticks, dat's all.
I'm very sleepy—upon my soul, (*yawns.*)

H. P. My contemptible liege—my royal sire—

King. Hush Mr. Priest, and at once retire—

H. P. But when, your insignificant majesty wakes !

King. Oh ! *ven* I vakes, dat anoder ting makes ;
But I don't vakes *now*, I do believes,
Or—ha—ha—mine eyes me very much deceives.
[*Exit H. P.*

[*The King, after making many preparations, blows his nose,
and lies down on the sofa.*

Enter HERR GENTLE BRUTE, *stealthily*, (s.)

SONG.—*Air, Comin' thro' the Rye.*

G. B. Oh ! if a pody meets ein pody
          Shleeping on de sophia ;
     If a pody kill a pody,
          Need a pody cry.
     Should dat pody be like a pody,
          Of ein King so seem ;
     Den if dis pody kill dat pody,
          Need dat pody scream.

     Oh ! if dis pody goes to dat pody
          Und shtabs him mit a knife,

* Head.

Can dat pody say to dis pody,
  "Shtop! you takes mine life?"
But if dat pody no say dat,
  Nor say no oder ting,
Vat keeps dis 'ere pluck shicken
  From killing dat 'ere king?

(*Recitation.*)

'Tis vell—yet not so vell I fear
As it might be; de King mit Lager Beer,
Is shicker* und sleeps; I must straight ·
Shtrip him of his power, and shtate—
Now, den, (*King snores,*) ah! vats de matter?

King (*asleep*).
  I now vill go, von taler better—
G. B. He shleeps his last dream—he fights his last war,
  And never he shall go von taler better any more,
  For shtraight I goes de deed to do,
  So King, down to hell mit you.
[*As he is in the act of stabbing, the King snores awfully.*
Herr Gentle Brute starts back in terror.

  Mine Gott—mine Gott—vat means dese tings,
  Dat in mine ears so loudly rings?
  Dere is more tings in earth und hell
  Den does in mine philosophy dwell.
  Herr Gentle Brute, be not so vomanlike,
  Und if a man—why for, de blow not strike—
  'Tis done—I am a man—and at once I—
  Hush—de King once more commence to cry;
  He has got a dreadful cold I tink;
  His voice so low in his nose does sink.

King (*asleep*).
  Mister High Priest it is understood,
  I'm two blind—do you make it goot?
G. B. Now is de bevitching time of de night
  Ven de poor peoples see by candle light—
  Und de rich, vy dey burns de pooty gas;
  Away! Philosophy—I let de goot time pass,
                [*Approaches, King starts.*

---

* Drunk.

Vat do I see before me—here—right here;
Is it not a glass of Lager Beer?
Come, let me clutch it—I have it not—
And yet it still is there by Gott.
De handle is to my hand, right here,
And now I look again—it is not beer,
But blood, some one mitin did pour,
Vich I know vas not so before!
Deres no such ting; to my surprise,
[Points to King.
It is dis bloody business, vich tells dis to mine
    eyes.
Thou goot ground, do not tell de King
That I will do dis bloody ting.
If you do, my goot ground you see,
The King might be very much mad with me—
I go, and it is done.
[Advances, and when in the act of stabbing, King wakes by
   the bite of musquitoes.

    King. Mein lieber Gott! vat's dis I see,
Herr Gentle Brute alone mit me?
Am I ashleep, or am I awake?
Mine Herr, how bad mine knees do shake!

    G. B. Shake! for it is de very last shake
Vich on dis earth you'll ever make.
Shake! you King, for never again
Vill lager beer befuddle your brain!
You've shook your shake, and took
Your time, now shake your shook.

        DUET.—Air, Matrimonial Troubles.
G. B. (aside).
    O tear, O tear, de King is awake,
And his life I no have take.
Vat shall I do—I'm in such a bad fix—
Shall I kill him, or cut my sticks?
King (aside.)
    Vat do I see mit dese two eyes?
De Gentle Brute, to my surprise!
I vonder for vat he does here?
Mischief to dis chicken I fear.

(*Aloud.*) Vat do you want Herr Gentle Brute mit us ?

G. B. To kill you, King ; so don't make a fuss.

King. I'll holler if you do it.

G. B. If you do, you'll rue it.

King. And if I don't, an't it de same ting mit me ?

King (*aside*).

       Vat do I see, etc.

G. B. (*aside*).

       O tear, O tear, de King, etc.

King. Now, please, Herr Brute, let's talk some sense.

G. B. No ; for if we do, it's at my expense.

King. Oh ! I'll pay, if it's lager beer you wish,

       And trow in a plate mid blind a fish.*

King (*aside*).

       Vat do I see mit, etc.

G. B. (*aside*).

       O tear, O tear, the King, etc.

G. B. To make dis tale a leetle short,

       I speak in earnest, not in sport.

       I come to fight—but not a duel—

       To kill you—say Shamai Israel.†

King (*aside*).

       Vat do I see mit, etc.

G. B. (*aside*).

       O tear, O tear, the King, etc.

G. B. Now prepare great King, to die,

       Your time is come, your hour is nigh.

       [*Col. Schwitzer peeps in and assures the King.*

King (*aside*).

       I vill prepare mitout a sigh,

       For I tink you tells a great big lie.

King (*aside*).

       Vat do I see mit, etc.

G. B. (*aside*).

       O tear, O tear, the King, etc.

(*Recitation.*)

King. Vat is your vish, and vich is your vat ?

* Blind a fish, a favorite dish among the Polish Jews.   † A prayer.

1*

G. B. To kill you, King—how do you like that?

King. Not a bit — vat's my offense — and vat's my
     crime ?

G. B. I'll tell you briefly, but not in rhyme.
     Scarce had de silber moont tree times
     Changed him's course, und only time
     Had I to drink two barrels mit Engel
     And Wolfe's besht Lager Beer, ven once
     Upon a dark, cold summer's night, caps
     For de head at night vas scarce, for
     None vas needed, as de sun shone very
     Bright ; it vas de most beautifullest
     Day (I tink it vas Rosh Chodesh Hallel,*) de
     Heavins looked blue all over, like mine
     Fader's Shabbes† coat, (ah ! he vas a great
     Man, and vore a long beard de color mit
     A carrot,) de earth it looked so green as
     Mine Vilhelmina's eyes—vell you, a rag
     Seller then, vas elected King—no more of
     That, for since that time, beer nor sausages
     Had any charms for me, and sour
     Krout, vich I like—ah ! once like so
     Very well, grew untasteful to mine
     Stomach—vell, you vas elected King—and
     Mitout one leetle thought uf mine claim
     To de crown, you put it on *your*
     Parech kopf‡—now, King Couple, are
     You satisfied ?

                  [*Col. Schwitzer again peeps in.*

King. Vat claim have you to dis pooty crown ?

G. B. A good one, tho' my name's not Brown.
     Now listen : My grandmoder, by my fader's side,
     Vas wooed by my grandad for his bride.
     After mit a long und happy marriage,
     One or two births, and a bad miscarriage,
     Mine fader vas born ; and *I* am his son.
     Is my claim goot ? My tale is done.

---

* Beginning of that month.   † Sabbath.
            ‡ Diseased head.

King. Cold and cruel-hearted subject,
    What can now be your object ?
G. B. To kill you ; for first *you* must die,
    And den—vy, I'll be King by and by.
King. Die ! ha, ha—now you shall see—
    The reward for your base treachery.
    One leetle vistel I now will give,
    And from death you shall no more live.
                       [*Whistles.*

Enter Col. Schwitzer, with the Francifoos† Guards,
*with three banners ; one bearing the king and queen
of clubs on it, with the word " Bella ;" one the nine
spots of clubs, with the word "Manell ;" and the third
having on it the jack of clubs, with the word " Yaas."*

G. B. The Francifoos Guards !
                    [*Aside.* Ah ! I understand.
Col. Schw. (*slapping him on the shoulder*).
    Yes ; and Col. Schwitzer is in command.
King. Col. Schwitzer, take the traitor hence ;
    I always said the Brute was on the fence.
[Herr Gentle Brute, after a desperate struggle, is seized.
G. B. (*struggling*).
    Unhand me ! my good shentlemens,
    Or mit your life you'll pay dis great expense.
                 [*Exeunt all but King.*
King. Mr. High Priest, come in here,
    And bring mit you a jug of beer.
[Enter H.P. with jug glasses, they seat themselves at table.
    Ah, mine goot poy, 'tis not such jolly ting
    For any man to be ein royal king,
    For though a king, I've a goot deal grief;
    But beer and shleep bring their relief.
               [*Enter Lord Luther Gab.*
Lord L. I come, most contemptible majesty,
    To join in your festivity,
    To rejoice with you, I now appear ;
 (*aside*) But more to drink some lager beer.
    I heard that your royal carcass was almost

       † A German game at cards.

On the eve of giving up the royal ghost—
Right glad I am.

King.   There, dat vill do,
We'll condescend to drink mit you.

[*Lord L. seats himself—King, getting lively, sings.*

SONG.—*Air, the Pope he leads a happy life.*

King.   De priest lives happy in de velt,*
IIe needs no wife—he needs no gelt ;†
De flock they give him meat and wine,
But *I would not like a priest* zu zein,‡
A chazan,§ it is goot to be,
IIe sings so sweet the melody.
Each Shabbes ¶ he gets a coogel ** fine ;
But *I would not like a* chazan zu zein,
I'd rather be a great Miloch,††
'Tis better than chazan or a galloch.‡‡
IIe eats, he sleeps, whenever he pleases,
Ven he takes snuff, his subjects sneezes.

Recitation.

Lord L. Good, good, your majesty sings well,
A voice, whose gentle swell
Vibrates on the air, and reaches—

King.   Vat yu mean by dese big speeches,
I cannot verstand dis high fallary,
Do you tink I am a valking dictionary ?
But Mr. high priest, vat for you appear,
So very much solemncoly here ;
Vat's turned up, or vat's turned down,
Dat you look mit your face so full of frown ?

II. P.   Nothing, nothing has happened to-day,
Which—

King.   Nothing makes nothing, dats what I say.

Lord L. A wise retort has your majesty flung—

King. (*interrupting*)
Lord Luther, just hold *your* tongue.
I have something mit importance to relate,

---

* World. † Money. ‡ To be. § A Jewish minister. ¶ Sabbath.
** Sabbath pastry. †† King. ‡‡ Priest.

Vat interests dis public and dis sthate;
 I dreamed a dream—
H. P. and Lord L.   A—dream!
King.   Vy, yes, does dat so very vonderful seem?
 I say, I dreamed a dream.
Lord L. A dre— [*King makes a gesture, and sings.*
  Song.—*Air, I dreamt I dwelt in marble halls, from the
  ·   Opera of the Bohemian Girl.*
King.   I dreamt I dwelt in a room you know well,
  With cards and with beer by my side,
  All present, which is not at all strange to tell,
  Thought of me, King Couple, with pride;
  We played poker, and had some very goot sport,
  Till I got four kings and an ace;
  When a knight, who hailed from Bavaria's court,
  Got mad and slapped my face,
   Got mad and slapped my face,
   Got mad and slapped my face.
(to H. P.) 'Twas then I called to you for to fight,
  But aid you would not give,
  You sided with Bavaria's knight,
  I could scarce my eyes believe.
  I then called aloud for Lord Luther Gab,
  Who pale and all trembling did seem;
  Lord Luther then quick gave me a stab,
   'Twas strange, though but a dream,
   'Twas strange, though but a dream,
   'Twas strange, though but a dream.

Recitation.

Vat you tink of my dream, shentlemens?
H. P. and Lord C.
  Wonderful!
King.   Ish—dat—all?—*uhm*, by Gott.
  I tink mit it some oder tought,
  I tink, though I am somewhat in the dark,
  "Someting is rotten mitin de State of Denmark."
[*A pause, while King walks with long strides, H. P. and
  Lord L. whisper.*
King.   Shentlemens! I tink shust now you said,

Dat de Muddy* brudders have arrived ;
If so it is, let him come and play,
Tho' I a little down to sleep will lay.
But not to slight dis mans of renown,
I'll leave mit you my robe and crown,
Vich is honor enough, eh, priest? vell I'll go
 along.

H. P.   The king, your majesty can do no wrong.
            [*Exit King.*

H. P. (*calling Lord L., who is about following the king*).

Lord Luther Gab, Lord Luther Gab,
Can I hold with you a short confab?

Lord L.   Aye, your excellency, as much as you desire,
Will you say it here, or shall we retire.

H. P.   This place will suit, 'twill answer very well,
Tho' what I now desire, Lord Luther, to tell,
Is of vast importance, I'll be sworn,
To us, and generations yet unborn.
You know the king, of him I speak,
Dont you think up here, he's rather weak?
His head *is* weak, empty, and soft ;
Is it as good on his shoulders as 'twould be off?

Lord L.   'Twould be no loss to us, as far as that goes,
Tho' a serious loss to him, I suppose.

H. P.   Wisely spoken ; but why should we refrain
From cutting off that, which to us gives no pain.
If you're the man I take you to be,
Your tphillim * hand now pledge to me.
Whatever I may propose or plan
Will suit, do you give me your hand?

Lord L.   Here is the hand on which I lay tphillim,*
       [*extending his left hand.*
It's yours, tho' the king, you desire to kill him.

H. P.   Thanks, in that promise King Couple smothers.
Lord L.   Hush ! here come the Motley Brothers.

*Enter lords, ladies ; then enter the Motley Brothers, who
go through many statuaries, representing the most*

---

* Motley.   † Phylacteries.

ludicrous positions and pastimes of prominent men;
after which they exit, leaving H. P. and Lord L.

Lord. L. Wonderful performances these, forsooth,
But, when I was young, ah, in my youth,
Few could vie with me, good priest,
At carnival, or at a feast.
To shoot a gun, or skillful row,
Or light upon the fantastic toe,
Or jump, run, sing, or write a verse—

H. P. You need not now your deeds rehearse.
Some vestige, my good lord, remains,
I pray you, therefore, spare your pains.

Lord L. True, true it *is* easy to be seen,
What a great man I once have been.
Say, high priest, am I right or wrong?
Though, to be sure, I still am young.
I'm not forty-five by full three weeks,
Besides, there's not a wrinkle on my cheeks;
A few gray hairs upon my head, 'tis true,
This must be kept 'twixt me and you.
            [*Exit H.P. unperceived*
But I know of men, ay plenty,
Who were gray at five-and-twenty;
Though men, governed by envy's rage,
Taunt and hint, and guess my age;
Yet the ladies all, upon my life,
Think me only twenty-five.
I could show — I sleep with them under my
    pillows—
Notes, which would betray a score of peccadil-
    loes,
Writ by hands of snowy whiteness,
Full of love and of politeness,
'Tis not my fault, good priest, I vow,
How can I remedy or help it now.
Nature made me attractive; if so it be,
Can any blame be attached to me?
Now listen, what I say to you,
Hallo—gone!—*he's* envious too.
                    [*Exit.*

END OF ACT I.

ACT II.

SCENE I.—*A Prison—Herr Brute seated on a bench, his hands and legs secured by long chains—he comes forward, and sings.*

SONG.—*Air, Something to Love.*

G. B. Nothing to eat in this world of sorrow,
    Nothing to drink in this world of care,
  I fear I shall starve before daylight to-morrow,
    If I am not fed on much better fare.
  I fear I shall, etc.

You'll all agree that King Couple's a villain,
    For he wouldn't let me stab him with my
      knife;
  The reason he would not allow me to kill him,
    Is because he's so fond of his miserable life.
  The reason he would, etc.

My luck is invisible, for it is so far off;
    You never have seen such bad luck before;
  I shall never again pray *Shachriss* or *Mahruv,**
    And never shake *Essrick* or *Lulew*† no more.
  I shall never, etc.

My stomach feels like I was on a ship or a
    clipper;
  I hope this bad feeling will not very long last;
  This is *Passach* ‡ 'tis true, but to me 'tis *Yom
    Kippoor*;§
  I vow, for three days I haven't broken my fast.
  This is *Passach*, etc.

All I own I'll bequeath, aye, every scintilla,
    For life at best is so frail and so brittle;
  I will leave all I own to some *Yidisha Killah,*¶
    Even to my silk *Tulliss* ** and *Kittell.*††
  I will leave, etc.

Oh! nothing to eat in this world, etc.

---

* Morning and evening prayer. † Palm and lemon, used on a certain holiday. ‡ Passover. § Day of atonement, or fast-day. ¶ Hebrew congregation. ** Four-cornered fringed garment. †† Gown used on certain festivals.

Enter WILHELMINA.

DUET.—*Air, Shells of Ocean.*

Wil. What's this I hear, my lover dear—
What's this I see, my lover here—
I know his voice, his voice I know,
It sets my heart and cheeks aglow.
His voice, my soul with joy it thrills,
With bliss *untold*, my heart it fills.

G. B. Oh ya! 'tis I—Oh ya! 'tis me,
Your lover true, mine Vilhelmincy—
I'm in de prison, mitout any hope,
And will be hung, mit my neck 'round a rope,
Den some oder Deitcher you will court.
And I as a *Vidow*, to de gallows be brought—

Wil. Ah! never again will this heart respond
To love; for once the heart thus fond,
That's clung to one, will cling forever,
And know joy nor love—Ah! never!
'Tis you I've loved—to you I've clung—
To you I'll *hang*—though you be hung—

G. B. (*recitation.*)
I'm glad I've met mit you, right here—
But did you come *alone*, my pooty dear?
You bring noting mit you eh? you know you
oughter,
I gets nothing here, mine tear, but bread mit
vater.
Vat's de use—I know you've brought someting
prime,
Now don't keep me in suspenders all de time—

Wil. I've brought— some beer!

G. B. Lager! I know it is, mine pooty tear.
Vat else?

Wil. Some cheese which cost me half a kreutzer.

G. B. Indeed! then I know it must be Schweitzer.

Wil. And Rye bread too, I've brought from home—

G. B. Oh! I'm so glad, my tear, that you have come.

[*Wilhelmina brings in a jug, glasses, cheese, bread, and
places them on a bench. G. B. seats himself, and
pitches liberally into the eatables and drinkables, after*

imbibing deeply of the latter, he gets unsteady on his pedestals, rises and sings.

AIR.—*The Red, White, and Blue.*

America's the country for me,
'Tis a land of great liberty,
Tho' hailing from Spain, or from France,
Even the Dutchman here, has a chance.
Goot sour krout you'll find here,
Goot sausages and beer,
Fine toback and vomen so pooty,
Good cheese, and fine gin toddy.
 Den hurrah for the goot Lager Beer
 Und hurrah for de Dutch sour krout—
(*To Wil.* From your looks, I tinks, mine tear,
 That your moder knows you're out—
 Den *hurrah* for the goot Lager, etc.
    [*Seats himself and sings.*
 De beer is the greatest invention
 Und Lager de besht in creation,
 Dis is very goot Schweitzere cheese.
(*To Wil.*) Anoder piece of Rye Bread if you please,
 I ask for nothing else from you
 De beer alone vill do.
 I vill drink mit your health in the glass,
 Und give tree big cheers as you pass.
(*rises*)   Den hurrah, etc. (*repeat*)
Wil. (*recitation*)
 My dear Brute, some accident,
 Or by some kindly angel sent,
 I found you—I'm prepared for any sacrifice—
 To release you, from here, at any price—
 Let future ages speak of what I'll do
 What will not woman's love tempt her to—
 Set her the task, and ask the boon,
 She'll snatch from Heaven the silvery moon,
 And lay it down before Love's shrine,
 And for love, her life resign—
G.B. (*tipsy*)
 Dat sounds mighty pooty I declare,
 I love to hear a voman curse and swear—

But though you swear once, or double
Swearing, won't get me out of trouble—
Wil. Teach me what to do, alas, I must be taught—
G. B. Shust vipe your nose, and shut your mouth—
Go to the King—you know him—hey, by jim.
(*aside*) I tink she has before made love to him—
Vell, 'tis no matter, first I'll get out here,
And den, vy I'll settle *your* hash, mine tear—
(*aloud*) Go to the King, and tell, if he vants to live
My pardon, he must quickly give—
But if he vants to die—vy dat's anoder ting, my
tear.
Be geshwind, I'm getting mighty impatient here.
[*Exit Wil. L.*

Song.—*Air, Bobbin around.*

G. B. My sorrows are so very great,
Is there no hope—no hope—no hope,
Must it really be my dreadful fate
To be hung by de neck, mit a rope.
I feel convinced, that I shall die,
Mine moder told me so last night
She would not tell her son a lie,
She told me this last night—
I sigh mit mine heart for grief,
In noting can I find relief
Oh! moder, my soul receive—
My sorrows are so very great,
Is there no hope—no hope—no hope,
Must it really be my dreadful fate,
To be hung by de neck mit a rope.
I know dat dese tings cannot last
—I'm very sad, oh tear—oh tear—
'Tis true dat I have broke my fast,
But want more beer—more beer—
I sigh mit mine heart for grief,
In noting can I find relief
Oh! moder, my soul receive.
My sorrows are so very, etc.,
(*recitation*) [*Enter High Priest and Lord L.*

G. B. (*tipsy*)
  Who goes here, mit such a noise,
  Is it some mans, or is it some boys?

H. P. No boys come here, Herr Gentle Brute
  Thy *august* presence to salute.

G. B. To me it makes no dif of bitterance,
  But it is *March*, not August, my goot shentle-
      mens—

H. P. We come to ask your doughty aid
          [*G. B. shakes his head and turns off.*
  For which—you will be well paid,
          [*G. B. extends his hand.*
  Will a dollar do? or two? or ten?

G. B. Did you say twelve thaler, my goot shentle-
      man?
  If such it is, and you mean vat you say,
  I'll do—but ven vill you the money pay?

H. P. As soon as you the deed have done
  Your pay shall, and quickly come—

G. B. Enough. I'm your man for any ting.

H. P. We want you to kill the king?

G. B. To kill the king? mit all my heart

H. P. Then go at once—play well your part—
    [*Exit G. B. after being released from his chains.*
      [*This can be omitted.*]

H. P. With plot, and strife, and discontent,
  The heart of man is daily rent:
  For what, I ask, is all this strife?
  To enjoy the few hours called life!
  The known world—aye, all creation,
  Is too narrow for man's ambition;
  And yet, a thick fog's gathering,
  A needle prick, a spider's sting,
  A leaden ball, a dagger's thrust,
  And man's ambition turns to dust.
  "This world is all a stage"
  So saith Avon's bard and sage.
  "And players all," poor mortals we,
  The Bard hath spoken truly.

Some men we see, whose only strife's
To play Rodrigo's part through life,
With pockets all devoid of cash,
With brains all filled with novel trash.
Sport Wisdom's cap quote Plutarch to the
  letter,
Folly's cap and bells would suit them better.
They utter another's labor as their own,
As if they had found the philosopher's stone.
Then there are men, shock-full of graces,
With false hearts and double faces,
Whose smooth and oily voice and tongue
Promise good to all, ill to none.
Their twinkling eyes all restless seem,
Poison lurks beneath that kindly mien.
Shylocks tread the world's broad stage,
For they are numerous in every age ;
Their souls for money are bought and sold,
They'd melt their God ! to bars of gold.
For *gold* they'd sell their very heart ;
Ah—many men play Shylock's part.
Now for the Ladies, they deserve a blessing,
Many play *their* parts at balls and dressing ;
There's the young miss—an acknowledged belle,
Know's nothing of a kitchen, but — sings and
  dances well.
She loves silly flattery, courts adulation
Hates reality, lives but in—imagination
Throws up her eyes with touching exclamation;
Her heart with silks is lined all through,
She loves romances, and believes them true ;
Sighs, not for miseries which round her dwell,
But novel miseries cause her heart to swell.
A glittering, painted butterfly, match for a fop-
  pish groom,
A fine piece of furniture for a drawing-room,
For dress and silly nonsense beats her heart,
And thus the tinselled belle plays her part.
I'd rather wed a devil—live in hell,
Than take to wife a city belle.

Now simpering, on the world's bright stage,
Comes the prudish lady of a *certain* age ;
'Pon her cheeks, ungallant father Time
Has marked the invidious aged lines.
But e'en Time's malice oft is baulked,
Wrinkles are easily hid and chalked.
What though the bloom of youth has fled !
The mysterious rouge is easily spread ;
What though the hair is turning gray,
Good *dye* will wash it all away ;
The limbs, 'tis true, are stiff at best,
Art and affectation must do the rest ;
Until she has entrapped her mate,
Affectation must amend her gait ;
And then, why *then* it doesn't matter,
She has got her victim in the halter.
The maiden of a certain age
Plays well her part on the world's bright stage.
And now the wife ; she comes with matron look,
The tempting bait no more upon her hook,
All affectation's is now forsook.
Whate'er her past condition's been,
She reigns it *now*, a very queen.
Though suds have dyed her hands—*now* fine,
And menial work has claimed their time,
All's forgot—must not be broached, or spoken,
Or you'll break her heart—which *now* is easily
    broken.
When wooed—how easy, kind, and pliant ;
When won—how independent and defiant.
Angry words and moody frowns,
Repay a quiet game at Brown's.
Where, now, the thrilling smile of greeting,
Which once a lover's heart set wildly beating ?
Where now the softened tone of voice,
That bade a lover's soul rejoice ?
All gone ; alas ! too soon it has fled,
With her maiden name 'tis quickly sped ;
With companions no more can he now loiter,
He's laid his *peace* on Hymen's altar.

But e'en such a wife, is not the worst,
With which, a husband's life too oft is cursed.
There be those, alas! who do not scold,
Though twelve or one the clock has tolled.
There be those, who not one reproach do say
To mates who spend their nights at drink or play.
Oh! worse—far worse, is their hapless lot,
When their very presence is thus forgot.
Novels too well requite the time,
They'll give up husbands, though not dress resign.
An absent husband, pshaw, it makes no differ-
    ence,
His money, too oft his *honor*, pays the expense,
But stop, old buster, you must cease these railings.
And speak of virtues, as you have of human
    failings ;
The dark side of the picture I have only shown,
'Tis time to show the brighter one—you'll own.
Of man—alas! for human nature,
I'll not speak of him, poor foppish creature.
Though one word let me say, in passing by,
Man could be great, if he'd but try.
'Tis true, that many men there be
In whom love of fame, and country,
Inspire no thought, no word, nor sigh,
Yet many, " were never born to die"—
Their names adorn bright history's page,
There live such men in every age ;
Woman! the dearest form, from earthly sod,
The noblest handiwork of God !
With her, man can brave the greatest ill,
Without her, lowly man were lowlier still ;
As maiden, wife, mother, in all life's parts,
She's a trump—for she's the ace of hearts.
Our waking goddess, the angel of our dreams,
She rules the warrior's sword and poet's themes ;
Without her, life were worse than death,
And death a hell—but I lack breath
To give praise to her, who rules in every nation.
God rules his creatures—*woman* rules creation.

Come cry with me, viva la bagatelle!
Long live the mother, wife and city belle.

SCENE 2.—*An antechamber of the Palace.*

Enter WILHELMINA.

Wil. (*solus*)—To the King I'll go, to please Herr Brute,
But other trappings for those occasions suit.
I therefore put on my new delaine,
And wear my golden rings and chain.
I have got on my bran new shoes.
Dress has surely dispelled the blues.
A few moments since I felt so sad,
And now—I don't feel near as bad.
Heigho—I know I love Herr Gentle Brute,
Though his nose, to be sure, don't exactly suit,
But his eyes are such a pretty blue, though rather
      small
'Tis true they twinkle like a Chinese ball.
But his heart—ah! that's indeed a prize
To make up for hooked nose and twinkling eyes.
Yes, his heart—that's true to the core,
What wants a loving woman more?
Heigh ho.

SONG.—*Air, Still so gently o'er me stealing.*—*From opera
      of Sonnambula.*

Wil. Still so gently o'er me stealing
      A curious sort of painful feeling;
      My senses all are strangely reeling,
        A sad pain hangs o'er me still.
      'Tis true no other man would harm me,
      Yet some other man might charm me.
      Now should some other ever claim me
        Will I love Herr Brute still?
      I think of no other man, when dreaming;
      Yet a ray of some waking thought is gleaming,
      Though I can not tell its pleasant meaning,
        Do I love Herr Brute still?
      'Tis true no other man, etc.,
      Heigh ho—what beautiful pictures, what a frame.
      I wonder, when married, if I'll own the same.

Oh! it must be a great and glorious thing,
To be a King—and *such* a King.
I wonder what he looks like—is he fat?
Tall he must be—I'm sure of that.
Full six feet ten, perhaps he is more,
IIis age, I'll warrant, is full three-score.
To meet him makes my heart flutter,
Not a word will I be able to utter.
Oh! Lord, here comes a man, I vow,
He's tall—majesty sits on his brow.
It may be him,—oh—I shall faint
May be it is the King—and may be it an't.

[*Enter Chamberlain.*

Chamb. (*aside.*)

A woman! does she come begging, I wonder?
She'll not get a shtiber of me, by thunder,—
I'll mind my P's and Q's, that clear.

(*Aloud.*) Halloo woman! what want you here?

Wil. (*aside.*)

That's the king—I know it by his voice.
Now for a speech that's both sweet and choice.

(*Aloud.*) Do I now address his majesty, the king?

Chamb. Woman! you now address no such thing.

Wil. (*aside.*)

' Woman! I never was called so in all my life.
What am I? his laundress, or his wife?
If impudence be the fashion here,
Two can play that game—that's clear.

Chamb. I am waiting, don't you see—speak your mind.

Wil. How can I see, when I've been so blind.

Chamb. Blind! what do you mean by this thing?

Wil. Haven't I mistaken the knave for the king?

Chamb. By thunder! woman, you surely rave.

Wil. No I don't, most august knave.

Chamb. Call you me knave, you witch of IIades?

Wil. Yes, the worst—the knave of spades—
You're that bull-headed, bow-legged, blear-eyed
card.

(*Aside.*) I think now I've hit him pretty hard.
Nothing will make a man more angry
Than the wounding of his vanity.

2

Chamb. (aside.)
       By Jove she's got me—how shall I act?
       I think I must somewhat change my tact.
(Aloud) Don't get excited, my pretty madam.
   Wil. I won't, thou ugly son of Adam.
Chamb. Why are you then so very snappish?
   Wil. Because you look so very apish.
Chamb. Tut—good woman, you're too full of wit—
       It won't advance your cause, no, not a bit.
   Wil. Indeed, you caused this sharp debate.
Chamb. Yes; but 't was only to appear great
 Wil. In *your* eyes, my lovely maid.
     (aside.)
       He's making love to me, I'm afraid.
       If that's the case, I'll bless the hour,
       That brought me to the palace-door.
       Not that *he* loves me, that's a disaster;
       But I might inspire a passion in his master.
       Oh! if I should!—hush! I'm watched—
       I count my chickens before they're hatched;
       But with the king to obtain an interview,
       I'll play the coquette and woman too.
(Aloud.) Pardon me, I'll not offend again
       Your noble ears, good chamberlain;
       'Twas but a whim—an innocent freak, you'll own,
       Which in a woman is by nature sown;
       Pardon, I pray, for had my tongue
       Obeyed my heart, I would have done no wrong.
Chamb. Love has surely played two parts,
       For at once he has smitten both our hearts.
       Come, my duck, let me twine this arm—
       Nay, I swear I'll do no harm.
Wil. (aside.)
       I didn't think of this, *(aloud)* good chamberlain—
       I would not for the world give you pain;
       But—but 'tis not modest, nor discreet,
       To—to—we're as it were, almost in the street;
       Just think, a curious ear, or prying eye
       Our strange position might espy.
       And then—then oh! good chamberlain,
       I pray, don't attempt this *here* again;

But quickly lead me to the king,
And then—why that's another thing.
Chamb. Ah! I understand, mum's the word—
What you say is not absurd.
Don't be impatient, I must first announce
A knight from a Bavarian province,
(I tell you this in strictest confidence,)
The king will first grant him audience.
When that is over—oh! you women,
I'll come back, and lead you to him.
Then I'll lead you quickly to the king,
And then—as you say—that's another thing.
[*Exeunt.*

END OF ACT II.

————————•●•————————

ACT III.

SCENE I.—*Audience Chamber of King Couple — King
seated on his throne—a Bavarian in a conspicuous place
in the apartment, bearing the inscription, " Rex Couple,
Dei Gratia "—High Priest, Lord Gab, and other noblemen
standing at the foot of the throne — Table, sofa, and chairs,
etc.*
[*Enter Chamberlain.*
Chamb. There waits without, a man all clad in steel,
Who has important matters to reveal.
King. Vat vants he? — und vat has he brought?
Chamb. A herald, sire! from Bavaria's court.
King. From our Cousin Ludwig! welcome he.
To Couple's court and country.
[*Enter Sir Arnold Doodlezack.*
King. Brave knight! (*aside.*) I like not his hair, or his
eye;
High priest, is he a herald, or a spy?
H. P. Our chumash* upon that point is clear :
It says—trust not men of reddish hair.

* Book.

Rashi* says : *Ani katager, nasas anager,*
Which means, being translated to this end.
" A bitter foe will never be a friend."
King (aside.)
    We'll try him (*aloud.*) Brave knight advance—
What news from Jerushaloyim,† or France?
Sir Arnold.
    I've heard that in the Holy Palestine
A rabbi's beard was severed from his chin ;
Which, when heard by the holy congregation,
Caused civil war throughout the nation.
Of France, sire ! — very little can be said,—
Rabbi Gamliel—ula vasholim ‡ —is dead !
King. Ah ! how long has the learned man been dead ?
Sir Arn. The shiloshim § are over, it is said.
King. Blest be his memory, — he was great whilst
    alive—ah !
France will erect a great matsivah ‖
Upon it his many virtues shall appear.
But brave knight, what vant you here?
Sir Arn. From my king I come — he needs the essentials,
        [*imitates counting of money.*
King. Hold ! first you must show us your credentials.

Sir Arn. (*whistles. Enter four pages, with brooms.*)
    Here are the emblems of Bavaria's court,—
They're the only credentials I have brought ;
But if further proof you should desire,
My king has told me, gracious sire,
To greet your royal ears with melody
Of songs from my native country.
King. Have you a voice, — can you sing ?
Sir Arn. They say so in our court, most gracious king.
King. Well, clear your throat,—what's the tune?
Sir Arn. 'Tis called and sung as, Buy a broom
      Song.—*Air, Buy a Broom.*
    (*Accompanied by a hand-organ.*)
Sir Arn. From Bavaria I come, with consent of mine
    liebshen,

* Great Commentator.   † Jerusalem.   ‡ Rest in peace.
‖ Days of mourning.   § Tombstone.

To the court of King Couple I come for to sing,
  Buy a broom, etc.   [*Pages wave brooms.*
To the court of King Couple I come for to sing.
The king, my master, who is not a joker,
Wants to be paid what you owe him for poker,
  Or by the broom, etc. [*Pages wave brooms.*
He will come here with his armies to fight.
    I now have delivered —

King (interrupting song.)
    Ah! did you say fight?
We will meet him by day or night.
He is much mistaken by mine beard,
If he thinks in *this* court he is feared.

Sir Arn. Two kreutzer and a half will stop this fray.
King. One kreutzer and two groschen is all we'll pay.
Sir Arn. My king says you'll pay more by-and-by.
King. Your king, bold knight, tells ein royal lie.
Sir Arn. But you —
King. Not another shtiber will we send— ⎫
  We'll meet him as a foe or friend— ⎬
  Our audience now is at an end. ⎭
Sir Arn. When Greek meets Greek, then comes the tug
    of war.   [*Exit.*
King, (to H. P.)
    Come; Ven Dutch meets Dutch, den comes de
    Lager Beer.

They seat themselves around a table and drink beer.

Enter CHAMBERLAIN.

Chamb. Sire! there waits without a fine lady,
  Who craves audience with your majesty.
King. Vell, let her wait until she's tired,
  Leave me at peace, is my desire.
Chamb. She's handsome, your majesty, and young,
  A voice like music—
King.   Hold your tongue.
(After a pause.)
    Vell, show her in to mine majesty,
    And—don't peep through de hole of de key.

[*Exit Chamberlain, and upon a gesture from King, exit all
  but King. The table is removed from the apartment*

King, (*solus.*)

> Some fools dey tink it is an easy ting
> For a man to be a majesty and king ;
> But very goot has de Bible got it down,
> Dat uneasy lies de head dat vears a crown.

Enter Wilhelmina ; she throws herself at the King's feet.

King. Shump up, shump up, my madam tear,
> All vat you say, we'll agree to hear,
> And vat you don't say, makes no matter.
> Get up, goot vomans ; it looks much better.

Wil. (*rises.*)

> O Sire—great King, and good,
> That you are kind, I've understood.
> I plead to you with trembling heart,
> And beg you, play a kingly part,
> Release *him*, pardon *him*, I pray.

King. Who is *him*, my pooty voman, say ?
Wil. Herr Gentle Brute, my lover dear.
King. He ! he ! who vanted to shtab me here ?
>   [*Points to his belly.*

Wil. He was to be my husband, is
> My lover.   Oh ! grant me this,
> And I will water your royal toe
> With tears, which from my very heart shall
> flow.

King. Vash mine toe !—an insult—vat you mean ?
> Do you tink mine feet is not vashed and clean ?
Wil. Oh ! noble Sire ! I would not dare.
>   [*Hangs down her head.*

King. You is—a very pooty voman, I declare.
(*With enthusiasm.*)

> " And if you love me as I love you,
> *No* knife shall shplit our love in two pieces."

Wil. Your majesty !
King.   Majesty no more,
> But adorer—for you I adore.
> Though very quick to you this love may seem,
> If you will have the king—vy you'll be *queen* ;
> A queen, not only of my heart and fate,
> But sole queen of my *vast* estate ;

A purse, which may be filled some of these days,
Two mules, a cow, and sixteen drays;
All these shall be yours, and, besides all this,
A set of *Rebunim Tphillim*,* and a *Taliss*,†
A wheelbarrow, drawn by a billy-goat,
My lovely queen through town shall toat.
You shall have oysters, clams, and brandy smash.
Say—won't my queen cut quite a dash?
Will you be queen? Will you have the king?
If so, your arms around me fling.
I have spoke mit feeling; have I said enough?
Will you be mine? Shall I say *mazzel toff?* *

Wil. (*aside.*)
My heart does with wild emotion beat;
I know not if I'm on my head or feet.
(*Musing.*) The king—Herr Gentle Brute—oh! my lot!
I look on this picture, then on that.
Herr Gentle Brute, must I thee desert?
Will not thou and history call me flirt?
Oh! my heart—my heart's so full,
My wits have gone a gathering wool.
(*Aloud.*) One moment for reflection, gracious sire,
Is all I crave—all, all that I desire.
(*Musing.*) As trifles light as air have altered stations,
Have created kingdoms, and ruined nations,
I'll now rely on these trifles of the air,
And sound names, and names compare.
Mrs. Gentle Brute—a common sound, I think.
Queen Couple—beautiful! Oh! I'm on the brink
Of—(*aloud*) Oh! yes, great King, I will be thine,
And Herr Gentle Brute at once resign.

King. Vell, I'll grant the Gentle Brute his life.
It would be mean to take his *leben** and his wife.
So come my queen, the Court shall know
The important tings vich happened shust now.
But hush! who comes now dis vay?
Do you know him, Whilhelmina?

* Phylactres used by a Rabbi. † A four cornered fringed
garment.   ‡ Good luck.   § Life.

Wil. (screams.)
>   Oh! 'tis the Gentle Brute,—he who owns a part
>   Of my dear hand, and dearer heart.

King.   Don't he frightened, mine pooty dear,
>   I'm your husband,—vy for you fear?
>   Come to mine arms; in them I'll hold you.
>   IIc can't do nothing more than scold you.

[*King takes her in his arms. Enters Gentle B., who starts.*

DUET.—*Air,* "*Barbara Allen.*"

G. B.   Am I deceived mit mine two eyes?
>   It is some hallu—cination,
>   If kings always talk with women so,
>   I be d—d if I like the fashion.
>   Vilhelmina, explain dis ting;
>   Is you for me, or for him?
>   If you be mine, vy 'tis all right;
>   If you be his—I'll floor him.

Wil.   Oh! Gentle Brute, why did you trust
>   Your bride with such a creature?
>   Look at his èyes and whiskers; oh!
>   An't that a lovely feature!
>   But don't be angry, Gentle Brute,
>   (These words are alone for you,)
>   I'll be a loving bride to both—
>   My heart has room for two.

G. B.   I'm in a rage—I am indeed,
>   But, by Josh! I'll trick her;
>   But first I'll drink some lager beer,
>   And get tremendous shicker.*
>   Then I'll come back, with glorious spunk,
>   All mine goot has turned to evil;
>   I'll come back —just mark my words,
>   And kick up the very devil.

Wil. (recitation.)
>   If you desire some lager beer,—
>   Sire? (*King assents.*) you shall drink some here.

[*Wilhelmina gets the beer, and throwing a white powder in it, tenders it to G. B.*

* Drunk.

Whil. It is Engel and Wolfe's best lager beer.

G. B. (*takes the glass.*)

> Very much obliged to you, *mine tear.* (*with sarcasm*)

(*Aside.*) Mien Gott, she is a very she tiefel.*

Wil. In this draught forget your rival.

G. B. Rifle! rifle! does you mean a gun?

(*Aside.*) This looks serious — it means no fun!

Wil. (*aside.*)

> The deed is done ; he drinks the liquor ;
> Soon he will be dead — not shicker.
> Epicac I've thrown within the glass,
> From earth, Herr Brute, you're going fast.
> His body will lie with only worms beside him ;
> His soul must go to Geinem or Ganeidem.†
> With a widow's cap for a while I'll be seen,
> And then—a crown I'll wear, as Couple's Queen.
> First, therefore, I'll sit shiva,‡ and then
> Queen Couple will be herself again.

[*Herr Brute, feeling the racking pain of the emetic, sings.*

Song.—*Air, Casta Diva from Opera of Norma.*

G. B. Oh! I bes so very sick,

> Someting here feels like, shust like a brick ;
> Veder it be de sour krout,
> Or some ting else, I know noting about :
> Oh! mine moder, vat can it be?
> Dat so troubles, troubles me.
> It may be de beer, de beer, de beer,
> Vat feels so heavy here,
> Or it may be de love dat I bear for de liebe
> Wilhelmina.
> Oh! yes, it is; oh! yes, it is dat;
> It is de Vilhelmina troubles me ;
> It is, oh yes, it is, oh yes it is
> Vilhelmina lays heavy on my chest ;
> Oh! yes, it is dat, etc. (*A pause.*)

* Devil. † Hell or Heaven. ‡ Mourning.

AIR : *latter part from "Oh ! hear me, Norma."*
Here in my fond heart,
 I feel such great pain,
I never shall live
 To see my life again.
For I know full well
 There was someting in de beer,
Or I couldn't feel so funny
 In my heart, right here.
It may be some pison ;
It would not be surprising
That she, de false one, she
Had killed and pisoned me.
  O me ! O me !
She would for do most anyting
To marry Couple de King.
Oh yes, most anyting
To marry Couple de King.
 De King, de King, oh ! oh !
  AIR, *Casta Diva.*
Oh ! I bes so very sick,
Someting on my heart, etc., etc.
G'. B. (*Recitation.*)
 Oh, shentelmens I die—I die !   [*Falls.*
(*To Wil.*)
But you, vill follow by and by—
Oh ! King, shust hear, what I've to say
Before mine soul does pass away ;
De High Priest and Lord Luther—Oh !
Are plotting for your overthrow.
Mischief to you we all did hatch,
Shust five minutes ago by de watch;
You know a man about to die,
Would not deceive or tell a lie ;
And what I now say is very true.
(*To Wil.*)
False one, I'm coming now to you.
King, Oh ! I've got such a pain in my stomach,
King, she don't know a word of Chumash,*

_____

* A book containing the five books of Moses.

She's got false teeth, and false hair,
As for her heart that's false I'll swear,
She shmells not so good mit her breath,
And she it is who caused my death;
More would I say before I die,
But can only say, goot bye—goot bye.

[Dies.

Wil. (to King.)
You don't believe one word he said ?
King. All—and more is true I'm afraid,
(aside.) Can I trust her ? she took his life,
She'll never do to be my wife :
But I fear that this mean baggage
Will sue me for a breach of marriage,
I'll kill her, that will stop her tongue,
As for the law—the King can do no wrong.

[Stabs Wil. who falls on a sofa.
So she's dead, I'm glad she's gone
She died without a word, or groan.
Ah ! here comes de Priest, and Mishter Gab,
I'm in no mood to hear mit their confab ;
By de bye, mit dese good shentelmen
I've got a bone to pick mid dem.

[Enter H. P. and LORD L., *they start on seeing the King
alive.*

King (aside.)
Treachery mitin their eyes is sticking.
H. P. to Lord L.
The King is still alive, and kicking.
(aloud.) Great King we come to greet you, and then—
King. To der Tiefel* mit all dis snigshalen,†
Herr Brute, who lies dead over yonder,
Told me tings vich made me vonder,
Said you were traitors, ere he died ;
H. P. Traitors ! King believe it not, he lied ;
And were he now alive, and not gone to dust,
The base lie down his Brutish throat I'd thrust.

---

* Devil. † Flattery.

King. Hush, Mr. Priest, I know you lie,
    I can tell it mit de vite of your eye,
                      [*Stabs H. P.*

    Quick, follow de Gentle Brute in his flight
    And you'll meet up mit him before de night.
                          [*H. P. falls.*
(*To Lord L.*)
    And as for you, the Priest will be very lonely,
    Follow quick, to keep him company.
            [*Stabs Lord L., who falls—a pause.*
King (seated.)
    Heins! bring some beer, mine majesty vants to
        drink.   [*a pause.*
    They all be deaf and Shtumm*, I really tink.
                         [*a pause.*
(*King knocks.*)
    Hallo! Shohn, cant you hear mine knock?
    Bring mine pipe, und bag mit Tobback.
                        [*a pause.*
The King rises and examines the persons lying around the apartment.

King. They are all dead, shust like a lump of stone.
(*distressfully.*)
    Mine Gott—Mine Gott, I am alone, all alone.

    Song.—*Air, I'm afloat, I'm afloat.*

King.
    I'm alone, I'm alone on dis grand mimic stage,
    The chairs are all empty, I'm alone in my rage;
    Though a King, a great King, I've no subjects to rule,
    And History will say, that King Couple's a fool.
    I call now for beer, and de beer is not brought,
    I'm alone in my kingdom, oh! terrible thought;
    I ask for obedience to my royal command,
    And none but the chairs my wish understand.

    I'm alone, I'm alone in my glorious state,
    I'm alone, all alone, oh! terrible fate.

---

* Dumb.

I'm alone, I'm alone, on this grand, etc., etc.
I am a great King, and have very fine laws,
My subjects are dead, I'm a ruler of straws;
The Kingdom of Couple is surely disgraced,
Its name off from History will soon be erased.

I'm alone, I'm alone in my glorious state,
I'm alone, all alone, oh terrible fate.

King (recitation.)
    All mine subjects now are dead and gone.
    And mit mine royal majesty I am all alone;
    I'm sorry tho' for mine goot high Priest,
    For he was so very jolly at a feast ;
    His loss indeed, gives me great pain,
    Oh ! I wish he would come back again.
H. P. (rising.)
    Have then thy wish, most gracious King !
                           [*King starts.*
    That I was dead was no such thing,
    Tho' heavy was your royal stroke,
    I only died, was dead—in joke ;
    Whene'er your majesty would fain
    Have me dead, I'll die again,
    In fun—
King. Dare, dat vill do,
    I'm glad I didn't shtick you thro' and through ;
    But what of them, is they dead for true,
    Or did they die in fun, like you ?
H. P. Music hath charms to tame the savage breast,
    You tried it on me, I'll try it on the rest.

    Song and Chorus.—*Air, We won't go home till
                   morning.*

H. P. (to body of Lord L.)
    Get up on your shanks, my good fellow,
    Get up, etc., etc.,
    Get up, etc., etc.,
    For it is the King's desire,
    It is the King's, etc.,
    It is the, etc.

Lord L. (rising.)
    I'm up and am ready, good High Priest,
    I'm up and am, etc.,
    I'm up and am, etc.
    If it is the King's desire.
Lord L. and H. P.
    It is the, etc.,
    It is the, etc.

G. B. I'm up mit mine shanks, don't you see it,
    I'm up mit, etc.,
    I'm up mit, etc.,
    If it is the King's desire.
G. B., Lord L. and H. P.
    It is the, etc.,
    It is the, etc.

Wil. (rises.)
    I obey with great pleasure the warning,
    I obey with, etc.,
    I obey with, etc.,
    If it is the King's desire.
Wil. G. B., Lord L. and H. P.
    It is the, etc.,
    It is the, etc.

King. De King is so happy mit you,
    De King is, etc.,
    De King is, etc.,
    So shust shtop dat music now.
[*Wilhelmina approaches the King to embrace him, he draws back.*

King.   (*recitation.*)
    I did'nt tink of this—*that* don't suit,
    Will you have her—Herr Gentle Brute?
G. B.   She's *too* much, for one poor subject,
(*aside.*)   To get rid of her, is now his object.
King.   Tame her, Herr Brute, it's an easy job.
G. B.   (*putting his thumb to his nose and spreading his fingers.*)
    Eh! No, sirree bob,
King.   Take her a leetle while, now do try,

G. B.	You sees any green, mitin mine eye?
King.	By Jove, I'll not have her, all alone,
	She won't suit mine subjects, nor mine throne,
G. B.	An't I a subject? You've spoken truly,
	For me she is a leetle unruly.
Wil.	Let me end this, all wise conversation,
	It interests you all, and all this nation,
	Since I'm too much for *one* of you,
	I'm not too much, I think for *two*,
	I promise both, upon my life,
	To be to each, a loving wife,

(*gives her hand.*)

	There, oh! King, and there Herr Brute,
	Does this, my proposition suit?
	What says, my noble liege and King?
King.	Vy vat you say makes anoder ting,
	That it suits me I'll frankly tell.
G. B.	And me it suits (*aside*) only tolerable well.

(*to King.*)

	You'll pay for her liquors, her paint, and her bonnet?
	Or I'll break the bargain, depend upon it,
King.	I'll do it mit the greatest pleasure,
	It shall be paid from the royal treasure,
	And now.

Song and Chorus.—*Air, Happy Land.*

Wil. Oh! happy hour, oh, happy day,
What shall I do, what shall I say,
Oh! I could sing, could dance and play,
We must be happy, must be gay,
Two lovers now, instead of one,
   Rich in charms and beauty,
Oh! I will have such glorious fun,
   Though to please both, will be my duty,
      oh-oh-oh-oh-oh-oh.

Chorus.

Oh happy hour, etc.

Wil.   Tra la la la la, Tra la la la la,
   Tra la la la la, Tra la la la la,
   Tra la la la la, Tra la la la la.

CHORUS.
  Let's all be happy, all be gay,

G. B.   Oh! happy hour, etc.
           She shall mend my shirts and night-caps,
             It don't make a bit of difference,
           And besides all her traps
             Will be at his expense,
                   oh-oh-oh-oh-oh-oh.

CHORUS.
  Oh happy hour, etc.

G. B.   Tra la la la la, etc.
                 Tra la la la la, etc.
                 Tra la la la la, etc.

CHORUS.
  Lets all be happy, all be gay,

King.   Oh! happy hour, etc.
           'Tis now agreed between us all,
             Let naught disturb our jollity,
           To-night we give a royal ball
             To all our grand nobility,
                   oh-oh-oh-oh-oh-oh.

CHORUS.
  Oh happy hour, etc.
King.   Tra la la la la, etc.
                 Tra la la la la, etc.
                 Tra la la la la, etc.

CHORUS.
  Lets all be happy, all be gay,

Lord L.   (*recitation.*)
           A ball! good gracious, I'm in such a flutter,
           Not a word of Chumash* can I now utter,
           Lets give hurrah's, one, two and three,
           To his great and generous majesty.
(*omnes but G. B.*)
           Hurrah! hurrah! hurrah!

---

* Book containing the five books of Moses.

(*II. P. slaps G. B. on the shoulder.*)
G. B.   Hoo-oo-rah-h !
King.   Silence !
G. B.   As a subject I obey,
        And have nothing more to say.
King.   Thus ends the eventful history
        Of the dark and dangerous conspiracy,
        Against King Couple and his reign,
        In spite of all, "*He is himself again.*"
        You see, there was no intention to kill him
        By Herr Gentle Brute, the principal villain,
        The killing, and plotting all was in fun,
        Our play, and our folly, both end in one.
G. B.   Not yet, a few words let me say,
        As a kind of epilogue to our play,
        Sometimes (it has been said, and wisely said,)
        'Tis right to put Folly's cap on Wisdom's head,
        Why should groans, and sighs, and sober looks
        Cloud our brow, as if joy had entirely us for-
            sook.
        If we were only formed for grief and care,
        Our lots would be " more than we could bear."
        Surely for this we were never created,
        Grief and God's mercy would be badly mated,
        Sages have said, " a little nonesense now and
            then,
        Is relished by the wisest men,"
        If a single line of care we have erased,
        Or conjured up a smile upon your face,
        We have been amply, fully been repaid,
        For all we this night have done or said,
        Too much our lives, in sorrows dwell,
        Too much of grief our bosoms fill ;
        And life, how short, how lone,
        E'er well enjoyed, is past and gone,
        Then why not deck our few short hours,
        With bright and sparkling, gems and flowers,
        When once our days are past and gone,
        Be they sad, or joyous, alas, 'tis one,

" For eyes that sparkle, eyes that weep,
Must all alike be sealed in sleep,"
What matter then, if *smiles* caress,
And hearts be filled with joyousness,
Or grief and frowns carve their traces,
On hearts, and cloud our faces;
Clap the cap and bells on Wisdom's head,
Let joy our hearts this night pervade,
Catch time by the forelock, say I not right?
Long live King Couple, and his doughty Knights.

CHORUS.

· Oh ! happy hour, etc.

Curtain falls.

www.ingramcontent.com/pod-product-compliance
Lightning Source LLC
Chambersburg PA
CBHW021445090426
42739CB00009B/1643